A 1000 Books of Poems

Volume-1

By:

Armando J. Nieves

Contents   Page

Introduction-------   05

Where Is Strength?   06

Self Destruction   06

Power   06

The Hour   07

Leaving The Life Behind   08

Hidden   09

Peace In The Sky   09

The Sharpest Blade   10

I've Got My Guns Ready But Where Do I Shoot?   10

Who Is It?   11

Turn The Mirror   12

Bad Company   12

Ms. Mary   13

Irony Of Man   13

Suicidal Thoughts   14

Poetic Justice   15

The Price To Pay   16

The Seasons Change, Yet Remain The Same   17

The Cycle   17

The Demon Below   18

The Cousin Of Death   19

The Eye Of The Storm   20

Eyes Within   21

First Of Love   21

---**Page**

Forbidden Fruit   22

Alive   22

Free   23

Happy Beyond Belief   24

The Black   24

The Master   25

Before, Beyond   26

Entwined   26

The Rose   27

Keep Going!   28

My Baby   29

The Tree   30

The Angel Of Mine   31

The Heart Of Man   32

History   33

Fear Of The Last Letter   34

Dead Presidents   35

Dream   36

The Blues   37

A Sun's Kiss Goodnight   38

The Vicious   38

Enchanted Beauty   39

The Jungle   40

The Wheel That Turns   41

The Three Fathers   42

Conclusion   43

Introduction

This is the first volume of many. The book is the compliment of love, hate trails and triumphs embedded in each and every page. This is history, thoughts, and many stories of what was seen, heard or lived. Most poems are short and the idea is to send a message in every letter and in every word. This book is meant to uplift and tickle the brain. There is nothing else but heart and soul from the cover to the back of the book, and I hope you will enjoy.

My Objective

I will not change the course of history
But the objective is to spark the idea in the light of a soul
For when that spark lights, it will change a nation
and the way they think and move
It isn't my duty to change the world
But it is my duty to spark the brain that will.

"Where Is Strength"

Man... The basic nature of men is to seek more power, and become stronger.

The irony of this is men look for power all their lives, yet true power is within him.

Inner strength, the most powerful part of a person. Which is only equal to the mind.

True strength comes from within.

When man learns this he will find that all the power is within himself.

"Self-Destruction"

Anger if harnessed correctly can make you strong

Hatred can make you blind

Rage can make you reckless and unpredictable

All of this is the spawn of anger

"Power"

A fight is not only won with brute strength, but with the mind with endless amount of potential and power which can overcome any obstacle whether it may be climbing the highest mountain or crossing the widest ocean.

"The Hour"

May I borrow what was once lost only 59 minutes ago?

Will gold suffice?

Will my soul pay the price?

Time taunts me as the clock ticks

Unforgiving for you only have one chance

Will my flesh suffice?

Is it possible to turn back once?

What price will I pay?

Thinking of tomorrow and not yesterday

May I turn the sands of time over?

Or will it turn me over?

In 60 more seconds my heart may go

When I pass, the hour will pass

Can I have another Chance?

To turn back?

To that that last hour?

"Leaving the Life Behind"

Cold is the heart is mine,
As steel touches flesh splitting the soul to oblivion
Darkness is the veil of silk
Overshadowing fear crushes faith, like heat burning desire.
Coward am I,
To take is death
To give is life
The truth is a lie
Yet the lie is the truth
The scar torn never-ending forgetfulness,
Water reminds and stares back
Sleep Walks
Open eyes stitched shut and barren heart
The blade pierces the heart
Not a single trickle
The mirror breaks
The new face
The shimmering smile of the glaring mirage
I have defeated me.

"Hidden"

The window is transparent, as murky water glides the surface

The illusion of the perpetual shine is the dim light of truth

The blanket of the night provides comfort, as the unborn in the womb

The moon shines, but there is nothing that can be seen

The stars point where his heart lies

Is it the mirage of love or the figment of hate?

The morning dew settles

The light creeps, like the thief in the night

The veil of lies is lifted

The eyes,

They can truly see it know.

"Peace in the Sky"

My mind wanders through the clouds

Trailing winds of reminisce

Dark clouds dampen the shine of the sun

Floating

Gliding

Slipping through the impossible thought

Nothing impossible

I return back to reality

All is clear.

"The Sharpest Blade"

Man should not fear any weapon
For if threaten by or used, pain will only be a moment
But yet the pen, men should fear for it may decide a man's
Happiness or suffering.

"I got my guns ready/But where do I shoot?"

As I walk down the street the sun glaring at my eyes

Smoke exhaling from chest, walking the narrow road

With many doors that now have locks.

Keys are hidden around, as I pull my weapon that may be the
key to unlocking all doors

My pistol is ready and I am always ready to fire, with unlimited
ammunition

With always, extra clips of knowledge.

"Who is it?"

It's midnight, an empty bottle of Jack and Dutch's at my side, as I daze and ponder.

The door knocks deeply, as I stagger to get to it.

I open it.

I see old grimly Death looking dead into my eyes.

Death speaks and says "Times almost up!" I look with a devilish grin and say "Maybe Tomorrow" and shut the door.

As I walk precariously back to search for another bottle, another rhythmic knock reaches my ears.

I open it

I answer and see young optimistic Opportunity

Opportunity speaks and says "Times almost up!" I laugh and say" Maybe Tomorrow" as I slam the door.

I go back to the living room grab a pen; the third knock aggravates my attention.

Once again,

I open it

I see none other than the reflection, yet I do not recognize

I stare

A revelation was upon me as perpetual thoughts flowed like water

Everything is still

But I sit and ask who is it?

But the real question is who am I?

"Turn the mirror"

Who are you that caused my destruction?

You are to blame!

For I am the one who refuses to turn the mirror on myself

I blame the creator!

I blame the men with lies in the windows!

I will blame all!

But the mirror I shall break before I turn it upon myself.

"Bad Company"

Cold and steadily growing like darkness from evening to night
As my heart grows heavy as kin has two faces
A fine line stands between the title of friend and foe
Confused am I to see with my third eye the truth
That is your right hand can cause your destruction as well as
your enemy
Can't trust no one
Not even me.

"Ms. Mary"

Born from the earth you sprout with strength and pride, knowing no hesitation as we greet you to ease my mind.

Relaxing my stress, and cut through pain like diamond on glass.

And though you take one form but many scents, with eyes closed I still recognize.

Even though times change you always remain the same.

I love you forever,

Ms. Mary

"Irony of Man"

Man loves tragedy,

Man loves battle,

Why else would man kill his own brethren?

For we all descend from the same table

Man loves anger, but forgets kindness,

Man neglects life, yet fears death

Man loves war

I laugh at the foolishness of man

Man loves to hate yet neglects love itself

I love the irony of man.

"Suicidal Thoughts"

In a dark room with a dim light, due to the darkness escaping through the crack of the door. I take a sip of the bitter taste that clouds my conscious. There is a revolver on the worn wooden brown table with one bullet. I rock back and forth in my chair thoughts racing, like stampeding horses around the track. My eye twitches though everything is clear. I am blind. I have lost everything. I finish the last of the poison in the glass, the shinny pistol glided smoothly like butter on toast in my hand. The bullet is loaded, along with the last cigarette to my parched lips. "What's left?' I say to myself, "No money, family, nothing!" My heart runs to fast that the body can't catch as I raise the revolver to my temple. I slightly squeeze the trigger; sweat shoots down my face like thunderbolts. I am shaking as a newborn terrified of the next move. My mouth becomes dry as a barren land and echoing voices encourage the intensity of the scorching flames. The laughter ascends throughout my body. My song in my heart stops and I finally muster the cowardice and pull the trigger.

Time freezes.

Was it worth it?

"Poetic Justice"

The law forbids treachery of a traitorous mind

The judge slams oak

Authority of might of the heart rules

Crushed to a million pieces of oblivion

Take back from the stolen

Revenge is yours to have

Leah, is times curse upon you

Wings are spread to fly

And forgiveness is mine.

"The Price to Pay"

No amount of gold is worth this

The world and anything is worthless

Pride averts

Hate converts

The soft rhythmic melody of the heart sings songs from the heavens

The soul cannot be traded but bonded

When two worlds collide

Unmatchable beauty spawns

But at what cost?

Nothing,

Everything,

For love has no price

But you.

"The Seasons change, yet remain the same"

Spring,
      Summers in
            Fall
Though what was once warm is now
                  Winter
Many don't Spring back into
                    Summer
For most are lost in the
            Winter.

"The Cycle"

From the first stone that was cast,

The crimson liquid created the lust of addiction

Life is given and Life is taken

The crimson gold that flows, caused the storm of chaos,

The crimson gold that shows, has a hold that eventually folds

Life is given and Life is taken

Crimson flames will always dance on the land,

The crimson is poison only by the heart of the motive

When the motive remains

The cycle

It remains.

"The Demon Below"

Locked in the cold, wet dungeon

Drooling of sadness

Self-destruction brews like morning dew

Stairs climb to a new world

The demon crawls from the embedment of emotion

Chains are broken

He climbs to the highest stair

The vortex of the new world is open

Eyes open full of fear

As others different yet same bask in ignorance

Shouting,

Taunting,

The angel appears with gorgeous emerald eyes

Her hand rescues his

Silence

They look at the mirror

The angel speaks" Come we are the same yet they are different"

Perpetual beauty stares back at the demon

All ignorant are ashamed

As they look in the mirror and see demons

The demon only sees angels

Beauty internal is eternal.

"The Cousin of Death"

The windows to the soul, drip slowly down

As light dims for ever shadowing darkness

Will is the weapon to ward off the crossfire of war

Strained am I, for if darkness wins it will prevail over the mind

Endless battle for an inevitable defeat

Swimming for lost untapped strength

This opponent cannot win!

Fighting back tirelessly

No Hope.

With the last stroke from my enemy,

I retire in peace

I sleep.

"The Eye of the Storm"

A single man who owns the ship in the vast open blue does not own the wind

Dark clouds blanket the sky as the eye envy arrogance of the man

The eye speaks" Leave this place for this place is mine"

The man replies," I am only finding what was lost"

The eye is filled with fury for the man has stepped on his foot with disobedience

The man ignores the eye and keeps searching

Freezing winds blow taking the breath out of his chest

"Leave" The eye shouts

And in seconds the boat is in the middle of a storm, with the eye watching

The man on the boat is getting tossed from the front of the boat to the back

The sail breaks

"I am not leaving until I have found what I lost"

The boat has a seesaw effect

And the man looks at the eye and says "Please! All I want is to find what is lost then I'll go home

The eye stares

I will give you one hour to leave then the storm will come to claim your life

The storm lifts instantly and Calm, fills the water and air

The mist depletes

He sees a familiar land

The man stares with a joyful smile

At Last

"Lost Within"

Sleepy, tired of awakening
Exhaustion of life within
Breath of life, exhilaration of death
On my feet but foot in grave
Strain thoughts of thought
Cowardice or bravery
Nap on the river
But still as the mountain
Careless as the wind
Where does it blow?
Wherever the streams go.

"First of Love"

My heart flutters as the butterfly
Fearful stinging of the body
Heartfelt stare, with mind aside
Shaking as the newborn
Breathless words speak
The beautiful forbidden flower of yours
Is the wine of mine
One heart
One soul
I will be yours if you let me
Forever.

"Forbidden Fruit"

From the earth you embellish
A magnificent seed
There is only bedazzled radiance
Of eternal light that outmatches the sun
When eyes are laid conviction of angels are formed
I am only a tenderfoot under your throne
Bless me with the touch of your bark
As branches bestow peace
The tips of your fingers are a sweet as the finest maple
Bless me with your benevolence
As I touch the fruit that only betrays my hate
And gives benediction of your love.

"Alive?"
I fall under
Light mist surrounds
White tile under my feet
Weightlessness fills me
Behind, the past
Ahead, blinding shimmering light
I fall deeper

I awake.

"Free"

I am the leaf that breaks from the tree

I dance with the wind

At a glance, you are stunned

At a stare, I disappear

You hear when I am near

You can catch me, only like the breath of love

I am nowhere to be found

But I can be found anywhere

I am the leaf that breaks from the tree.

"Happy Beyond Belief"

The heart frolics though the field of roses

Pedals dancing

Circles of warmth from mother's chest

Strings of harp tingling the senses

Crisp breath

Open, locked box

Life anew.

"The Black"

I am the hole that swallows the spirit
The one who robs pride from the heart
I am the void of confidence
You feel when I am near
I come from the shadows
Constricting power within
Binding strength of thought
I manipulate
You give me power
For I am
The Black.

"The Master"

The master moves without stagnation as the ocean

The master is facile in the extravagant slink tempo as the blues of the sky

The master controls the willing and the unwilling

The master heals wounds

The master inflicts wounds

You may love her

You may hate her

But time has no master.

"Before, Beyond"

Transparent walls,
Cracked glass,
Crumbled roof,
No beginning,
No ending,
Soul scarred
From the blades of the hands of the clock
Decapitating, Lacerating
From the inferno of reminisce

"Entwined"

Tired hands, unable to grasp
Worn feet, unable to hold still
Head, unable to lift
Body, unable to turn
Will dwindling,
Hope rising,
Climbing the mountain
For we are two,
Finding again to be one
I am lost without
You.

"The Rose"

Through the flames of hell,
And swoop of infection,
I climb and I grow
Though the mountains crumble
And the rivers dry,
I climb and I grow
Even when the ground shatters under my feet,
And others may say I am too weak
I will continue to climb and continue to grow
Even when they say there is no love and no hope
I cope
And on this final day
When they said I will fall and cease to grow
I blossom above all to see.

"Keep Going"

Through the cracks of the concrete
I hold my head up
Through rainy days and dark clouds
I hold my head up
Even when the earth shatters beneath my feet
I hold my head up
Even when the world is on my back and I eat the dirt
I hold my head up
Even when the mountain is too tall and the ocean is too wide
And the sky seems endless
I just keep on
Keepin' on
And my head is held high.

"My Baby"

The seed is planted in the soil

It matures with love

Roots sprout, fighting the dirt

Storm drowns the seed

The seed lives

Fighting the dirt and water

The seed grows climbing, but not knowing how far it has to go

The thunderstorm arises and destroys almost everything

The seed lives

Fighting drenched soil and tattered roots

The seed grows climbing, but not knowing how far it has to go

The brim of soil cracks, light shines

The hurricane comes

Nothing lives

But the seed lives

And in the aftermath

The seed rips through the dirt like the ruggedness of ravished love

And atlas the small fragile stem is born

And on it

A leaf

Simply Beauty.

"The Tree"

The center of the tree startles the mind

The branches cease to move

Yet the fruit is as sweet as sugarcane

The center of the tree, if it bleeds

There will cease to be seeds

If the bark is cold

The tree will quickly become old

The warmth of the center feeds

For that determines how strong the roots will be.

"The Angel of Mine"

You descend from the heavens

You are the embodiment of beauty and elegance

One look can stop war

One touch can soften the hardest heart of stone

One kiss can uplift

You are the pride innovation of God

The brightest star

The masterpiece

My angel.

"The Heart of Man"

I am the evil that lurks around you day or night

I am the flames of despair born from hatred

He is my brother but we are one

I am the calm before the storm, to whom I show my love is my choice

I may kill or I may love, help or let you go

I have no face but everyone knows who I am

If I had a chance

I would cut you and leave you in pieces

If I had a chance

I would love you and hug you no matter the circumstance

I hate you

I love you

Who am I?

The heart of man.

"History"

The redundancy of ignorance befalls a nation

The most powerful, yet the most vulnerable

Closed doors

Locked windows

Open to nothing

Open to arrogance

Stupidity is the aura

Minds sunken

The foolish rivers of deceit is home

The repetition must stop

Before all is lost

And nothing is won.

"Fear of the Last Letter"

Songs ring from a distance

Drums take my lead

Chains of binding vines are broken

Forward is the destination

The sight of tomorrow is a faint blur

Today is as the weather

For if rain pours my armor will rust

If the wind blows my sword will be one with the breeze

And if the ground is as unsure as the sea

My boots will surely fall through

But if this is the day my home is the grave

I will not lie

For even if the earth is on top

My head will be held high.

To My Love

"Dead Presidents"

Souls are sold for the dead tree

The ultimate price for death to be free

Too many with open eyes but cannot see

Selling something for nothing

But not me

For I miss thee

And hope heaven is my residence

Sadly to see no family and no friends

Because they sold their soul for

Dead Presidents.

"Dreams"

Stars cut through the sky like sickle to barley at day
Clouds play showing what isn't there at night
Birds swim
Fish fly
Up is down
Left is right
Actions speak
Words silence
Truths never lie
And lies are never true
Life is the many rivers that return to the sea
I fly
But I cannot
I am blind
But I can see
Simply
The grave is where you find peace
Death is the beginning and
Life is a dream
Within a dream.

"The Blues"

Stories told unwrapping the present of last year
Smiles and Cries
Happiness and Fears
The hand that brings joy
And the blade that brings a tear
What words cannot say
The sax sings
Through this long maze
That puts the mind and heart at a daze
At the end of these days
Feelin' blue or feelin' true
That is the embodiment
And the essence
Of the Blues.

"A Suns' Kiss Goodnight"

The weary sun tired of work closes his eyes
Lightly cursing the pure white sand
Grains walk across the peace of the shore
Short breaths of air soothe the skin
As the sprays cool the warmth of the sun
Life shows itself briefly above water
As the relaxation of the parting sun, leaves a moment of tranquility.

"The Vicious"

The monster gently manipulates the heart
Grasping the love
Drawing in
Cuddling the soul
Then ripping the heart
Embedding scar's on the soul
Shears of thread broken
The last straw is pulled
I will be scarred no more
For I am the stronger woman now
So be gone
The Vicious.

"Enchanted Beauty"

Emerald leaves trickle down from the wise trees

The sweat calming lavender settles the soul and tickles the nose

The shimmering light reflects passion of life from the water

This elegant place has seen many of days

With young soul and open heart

When the last sun sets

Hope only bathes

To see again

As I walk through

The enchanted perpetual beauty

Of

The Forest.

"The Jungle"

Heat crashes down
As sadness droves through cracked concrete
Broken hearts lay on the sidewalks
Dreams are found in the gutter
A forgotten place
Where souls leave no trace
Empty shells sit on broken crates
With fractured minds
A place where hope is unspoken
The deadly maze where few make
The never-ending trails to escape
From
The Jungle.

"The Wheel That Turns"

The wheel rolls
Nothing stands in its way
Rolling past
The desert
The mountains
The jungle
The forest
It was said the wheel would stop
But it rolled past disbelief
The wheel rolls
Nothing stands in its way
Nothing is too big for the wheel to roll over
As the sun and moon turns
The wheel turns.

"The Three Fathers"

There were three fathers. On the good day an omni powerful entity came to them .The three fathers were friends and all wanted one thing that thought to make them happier.

On the good day the entity came to them and spoke "You have been chosen to be blessed with one thing to make emptiness in your heart". The first father smiled with unwavering happiness and asked for money. The second father had a devilish grin and asked for power. But the last father calmly wished for infinite wisdom. The two fathers laughed and said he was foolish. The entity waved his hand and the wishes were granted. Then the entity disappeared. Three months later, the father that wished for money had spent it all. The father that wished for power had eventually diminished. But the last father used some of the money from the first father who threw it in his face, started a business and used the second father's power for public relations and became successful. Now the two fathers happily worked for the wise one.

Karma is God's Sense of Humor.

Conclusion:

I would like to thank everyone who took their time out to read this book. I appreciate your thirst for poetic genre and hope you to will chase dreams of your own. I only hope that the simple words I use touch a soul to overcome adversities and stands for what they believe in. I will also like to thank the two most important girls in my life that caused me to write again. And finally I would like to thank everyone who said it was possible and especially those that said it was not. If it wasn't for doubt there wouldn't be confidence, and if it wasn't for hopelessness there wouldn't be hope.

<u>Thank You</u>

Last But Not Least

The conclusion is only the beginning of a new
chapter

After death there is life

After life there is death

It is not how long life last

But only how it is lived

For the river returned from whence it came

    And by far

        I'm' aint finished yet

P.S.

Everything Starts With Thought.

My Name is Armando J. Nieves; I was born February 16, 1989 and raised in Miami, Florida. This is "A 1000 Books of Poems". Yes, there will be a thousand volumes with estimated 50 poems in each volume. This book is filled with a combination of love, hate, rising and falling among others. This book is written for the sole purpose of self-expression in the hopes of others expressing themselves. This is the first volume. There are still 999 more volumes to go, and I hope you enjoy reading it. Thank you Leah and Mia for I wouldn't be writing this if it wasn't for you. God First. Thank You

"The Journey"

Life, the only thing that cannot be fully explained with just words. Every time a life passes, there is life anew. My experience to see a seed blossom into a beautiful flower can fill warmth to the coldest heart. The natural essence of the process is as long and can be just as treacherous as navigating to a place that was thought not to exist. For nine grueling months before the seed is a flower it is put through various difficult and life threatening tasks. I only wish I could grow for her, for the womb she was in was rejecting her, fighting her off as if she was infection.

The mother was grief stricken to find news of the obstacles of trisomy 18 that would surely destroy her. Tears trickle as if my face was a desert and was in thirst for rain.

There were more than obstacles to overcome. During the pregnancy the stress of a stillborn infant clouded the happy thoughts of birth. This is, however the beginning of the downfall of the mother's body. In the middle of the pregnancy she developed "Help Syndrome"; which is elevated liver enzymes, and Low Platelets. Preeclampsia was also initiated throughout the body and basically made a furnace for the baby. All seemed dark and dreary, "but in darkness there is light".

The temple that was holding the baby was rapidly fracturing and it seemed as if the supporting columns were failing. At the last stage of her pregnancy a baby shower was meticulously organized. This is however, a dream she was not meant to see; because six days earlier the doctor requested her to come to the hospital. When she arrived at the hospital she was admitted and placed under 24 hour surveillance. The baby shower was as big of hit as a sold out concert, but sadly she wasn't able to attend though she had backing and support of a diehard fan and a football team.

Finally, the moment of truth was quickly occurring and the countdown was speed up one month in advance. All preparations were met from special physicians, to expert nutritionist's and the time was now.

Mental and emotional preparation had to be the last and final grueling obstacle to face. With a deep breath and faith the baby came out with an umbilical cord wrapped around her neck causing respiratory malfunctions. Fear hit me like a bolt of lightning, but with the first sound of breath and a loud echoing shriek, ironically only relief bathed over me like steam in a spa. Wailing and searching for the love that was in her first home, we gazed in her eyes and could only say one thing "Mia" and welcomed her with open arms and an unsteady confidence that comes with being a new parent. "Thank God, she is healthy ".

www.ingramcontent.com/pod-product-compliance
Lightning Source LLC
Chambersburg PA
CBHW070111070426
42448CB00038B/2512